EFFECTS AND TRICKS

EFFECTS AND TRICKS

PAINTING

TEXTURES

AND VOLUME

JOSÉ M. PARRAMÓN

Overall manager: José M. Parramón Vilasaló
Texts: José M. Parramón and Gabriel Martin
Editing, layout and design: Lema Publications, S.L.
Cover: Lema Publications, S.L.
Editorial manager: José M. Parramón Homs
Editor: Eva Mª Durán
Original title: *Pintando texturas y volumen*
Translation: Mike Roberts
Coordination: Eduardo Hernández

Photography and photosetting: Novasis, S.A.

First edition: April 2000
© José M. Parramón Vilasaló
© Exclusive publishing rights: Lema Publications, S.L.
Published and distributed by Lema Publications, S.L.
Gran Via de les Corts Catalanes, 8-10, 1º 5ª A
08902 L'Hospitalet de Llobregat (Barcelona)

ISBN 84-95323-35-4
Printed in Spain

Table of contents

Introduction, 6

1

Fig. 1. Venetian tabolas *by Gabriel Martín (artist's private collection). Sticking pieces of paper one on top of another gives the painting a layered appearance as well as an interesting colored background for painting over.*

Fig. 2. Xemaá-El-Fná *by Miguel Olivares (private collection). All of this artist's work was based on the interaction between sticky paper and paint. It augments the wrinkled surface and the effect of volume that it creates, producing paint with a more tactile composition.*

2

Many books like this one, which aim to teach how to paint, neglect to explain fundamental facts concerning materials and how to manipulate them properly. It is not enough to merely have artistic perceptions, you should also know how to interpret correctly. Technical advances with respect to paint and the appearance of new materials allow the artist to create new types of effect and quality that add a new interest to the surface of the painting, extending the potential of the artist's palette. Different artists use different methods, adding a creative dimension to the artistic process, something which is not always possible in more conventional fields. Therefore, art must be explained through the materials, procedures, tools and techniques that will lead the reader towards the representation of what could best be described as tactile paint, raised work with relief, or the process of producing the most widely known forms of three-dimensional surfaces.

The technique of painting in relief is not a new one; it has been a popular style for many years now. Thick pastes of oil paint were used during the Baroque period and more recently, in the 20th century, in Dadaist collages and in the materialist paintings of the Informalists, who made the surfaces of their paintings more interesting through the use of thick paint, adherent bodies and incisions. It was one of

Fig. 3. Bunch of flowers *by Teresa Trol (artist's private collection). Pasting is one of the most direct and possibly most popular methods of creating relief on a painting surface. It lends the painting an interesting expressionist feel.*

Fig. 4. Il sole c'e con me *by Teresa Trol (artist's private collection). Any material can be stuck to the surface of a painting to produce a feel of relief and volume. In this example, the artist has used small pieces of wood to get this pleasant and original composition, far removed from the flat appearance that paint usually has.*

Fig. 5. Composition *by Teresa Trol (artist's private collection). Any element can be stuck to the surface of a painting to suggest volume. In this case, the artist has used plastic with air pockets to act as a base for this abstract composition.*

3

Introduction

these, the French artist Jean Dubuffet, who said the following about material paint:"...he who believes that these pastes (paint with relief) are inactive, is completely wrong. Shapelessness does not imply inactivity... My relationships with the materials I use are like those of a dancer with his partner, of a rider with his horse, of the fortuneteller with his tarot cards. So it is possible to understand the interest that I have for a new plastering material and my impatience to try it out."

And this is the key: the interest that the artist feels towards these new materials and the need to experiment with them. You need to develop that same kind of interest, and follow these same paths of experimentation as you fill your paintings with the different techniques that are examined in this book.

The main aims of this book are to clear up doubts, suggest ideas and encourage the reader to move away from the traditional focus of conventional painting and to tackle alternative methods. As you will see, there are plenty of techniques to be found in this book, and many of them are far from well-known (such as painting with silicon or molding with plaster), and others are rarely used but nevertheless extremely interesting (encaustic, textures with organic elements and painting on glass), while others are far more common (oil pastes, acrylic pastes and collages and

5

mediums with tissue paper). The reader will discover materials that he may have never related to art before, but will find that all that's needed is a little inventiveness and an open mind to be able to combine them in the creation of a three dimensional painting surface.

If you apply the techniques that are presented here, you will learn how to see your model in a different way, to use your imagination, to reinterpret the way in which you perceive things, and to develop new textures and effects that are not usually considered but which make your pictures more interesting. This manual should be of interest to all those people who are interest-

ed in understanding the most common mixed techniques that are in use today. There is a wide range of different ideas, and anyone can choose the ones that most appeal to their own temperament.

The styles used by the painters who have carried out each exercise also vary, along with their different moods and interests. But they all have one thing in common; they are masters of textural effects, molding and pasting, the skills that are needed for creating a three dimensional surface. As you will see, each step-by-step exercise is accompanied by useful advice and models painted by famous artists, which serve as handy references and point your own particular search for the right images in the right direction. Familiarizing yourself with the basic processes of painting relief will open the door to fascinating projects, and the idea of combining each of the different mediums explored herein will lead you to even more original discoveries.

Gabriel Martín Roig
Art critic

4

Pasting with paint

Pasting, or *impasto*, as opposed to veiling, is the technique of applying thick paint as abundant layers of color over the canvas so that the brush-strokes are completely visible and create a textured effect. Its application creates a clumsy, irregular surface with crests and gaps on which light and shadow produce patterns. Thick, free layers retain the marks and forms of the brush on the surface of the picture. Pastes can be described as light or deep, depending on the amount of color that the artist applies to the canvas. Pasting can involve the mixing of two or three colors on the end of a brush, producing grooved strokes that reproduce the lines of the bristles. This is often done by applying thick color over a damp layer of paint, and the brush mixes the two colors on the painting surface.

When the mixture has been made in a purely free manner, the different colors are both together and separated in the same stroke, creating a lively sensation.

Paint is either taken straight from the tube or diluted with a little medium to make it more malleable, but still thick enough to hold its density on the actual surface. Oil paint has a unique texture that has enough consistency to create particularly dense pastes. On the other hand, acrylic paints are more fluid and need a gel or thickening agent to get enough body.

The paste can either be made with a brush, with a spatula or even be produced directly onto the surface of the painting. Pastes made with a brush

Fig. 1. **Floral composition** *by Teresa Trol (artist's private collection). Colored pastes can be used as part of any composition, from a landscape with dense vegetation to a still life like this. When we paint flowers with pastes, you need to control the direction of your strokes carefully. Simply applying color is not enough, your strokes need to follow the rhythm of the composition (for example, radial strokes are used for the petals, and the stalks are painted upwards).*

Fig. 2. **English garden** *by Carlant (artist's private collection). The use of a spatula is more common than that of a brush. Although the image looks rather rough, unclear and bereft of detail, the impact of the color that its use creates is full of interesting effects.*

Fig. 3. **Uçhisar** *by Josep Antoni Domingo (artist's private collection). Acrylics, like oil paints, are an ideal medium for pasting techniques. However, they do tend to dry rather quickly. They are unsuitable for outdoor work because if they are exposed to sunlight they dry even faster.*

have a uniformly thick surface with rich, varied lines in short, solid and grooved strokes. Those made with a spatula are more irregular and pasty in appearance, with a more geometric layout due to the flat edges of most blades. When we apply acrylic paints directly from the tube, the lines of paint have a marked volume that contrasts with the flat surface of the support (this is known as the extracted technique). Work with a spatula is definitely produces the most evident effects, because the scraping of a spatula allows for several types of paste and consequently a wider range of textures in one given area.

In paintings that use thick pastes of color you need to consider the option of mixing directly onto the surface as well as just on your palette. Sometimes, a tone can be corrected by adding color directly. Pastes can be combined with veils to create several interesting effects, because diluted paint sinks into the gaps and does not stick to the whole of the relief area.

5

4

6

Fig. 4. Sunset *by Óscar Sanchís (artist's private collection). Gel is a thickening agent that adds more body and volume to acrylic paints. Such striking compositions as this Caribbean sunset can be produced by pasting.*

Fig. 5. Interior garden *by Óscar Sanchís (artist's private collection). The impact of thick color applied with a spatula creates dynamic, textured paintings. Spatulas are useful for applying colors onto a wet oil surface without darkening the color underneath and for shaping the paint as it is spread.*

Fig. 6. Floral composition *by Teresa Trol (artist's private collection). The graffito technique is closely related to pasting. While pasting puts color into a piece, graffito produces graphical expression in the perfect combination of color and lines.*

Collages

The collage technique, a word derived from the French *coller* (to stick), involves sticking fragments of heterogeneous material (paper, cloth, wood, twigs and so on) onto a support (be it cloth, cardboard, canvas or any other surface), and then structuring them by freely choosing different forms, colors and qualities. A collage takes advantage of the different contrasts between the forms, colors and textures of different materials.

This technique became most widespread with the arrival of cubism, and thanks to artists such as Picasso, Gris and Braque it became extremely popular. Since then there have been many artists who hold a strong regard for the manipulation of materials and the intervention of a random element in art.

These artists have used the collage as a formula for stimulating creative inventiveness. In the second half of the 20th century, when traditional oil paints were considered somewhat old fashioned, several artists such as Matisse, Malevich, Severini, Schwitters, Arp, Haims and Dubuffet became famous for their use of collage techniques in their work.

Once the possibilities of the collage have been understood, you should experiment with the different materials that will determine the methodology you are going to follow. Many Dadaists included certain objects in their collages based on their associations or what they may represent. These *objects trovés* (found objects), allow the artist to create compositions that are just as interesting as those made using more traditional methods. More recently, Informalist and Neoexpressionist painters have been known to stick organic elements into their work to produce more suggestive and attractive textures. Excessive consumerism and the modern need for recycling have left the artist in a very favorable situation, because most disposable objects can be attached to canvas to add structure to

Fig. 1. **Still life** *by Bibiana Crespo (artist's private collection). In this collage, pieces of paper stuck on the surface play an important compositional role. In collage work like this, it can be interesting to combine paper of different qualities and textures. Look at the difference between the colored cardboard and the piece of newspaper.*

Fig. 2. **Enninskillen** *by Gabriel Martín (private collection). If brightly colored pieces of paper interact in a collage, the image will seem livelier and more vibrant. A collage is usually combined with paint to lend an image that linear reference that is so important in an urban scene like this.*

Fig. 3. **The bank of the Nile** *by Óscar Sanchís (artist's private collection). A collage does not necessarily have to be flat; you can also make relief and texture on the surface. Screwed up tissue paper can make a perfect irregular surface for simulating the cracks and grooves in a mountainside.*

collages. This is just one example of how materials can be reused to the artist's advantage.

Through making collages, you should find that you are able to produce pleasant, stimulating compositions without worrying too much about reproducing the forms and volumes of the model too accurately. A collage can be as simple or as complex as you like, it can be abstract or figurative, realistic or purely decorative, it can be combined with paint or can be made up purely of the different fragments. The collage is an experimental medium for which there are no strict laws.

The construction of relatively complex three-dimensional objects derives from collage ideas. Acrylic mediums have excellent adhesive qualities and are therefore ideal for sticking materials onto, even quite heavy objects will hold fast when stuck onto the support. Whichever type of collage we are making, it is often a good idea to combine it with other procedures. Compositions made as collages are extremely useful for recapturing an impression or as a compositional exercise, but if we want to use it to the maximum of its capabilities it is often a good idea to finish off your work with a little painting in the most traditional sense of the word, thus combining two very different styles in one composition.

4

5

6

Fig. 4. Composition with leaves *by Teresa Trol (artist's private collection). Any stroll in a wood will supply you with interesting organic materials to stick onto your support. The resulting compositions will be attractive and effective.*

Fig. 5. City of Lugo *by Gabriel Martín (artist's private collection.) A collage is an excellent chromatic complement for drawings like this. Notice how the chalk lines so perfectly combine with the pieces of cardboard that appear juxtaposed.*

Fig. 6. Flowers *by Teresa Trol (artist's private collection) Ephemeral materials such as twigs and leaves can also be included in a picture to produce such interesting results as these.*

Solid additives

Painting with solid additives involves adding powdered or ground materials to the paint so as to create textured or granulated surfaces. Paints that contain such materials can produce very differ-

ent effects to those that are produced by paint taken directly from the tube or applied as pastes.

The best way to get used to painting with paints modified in such a way is to begin with those agents that, when added to oil paints, produce regular textures and a guaranteed mixture, such as, for example, wax, pumice stone, ash, clean sand or sawdust. When using acrylics, you should use latex. These mixtures can be exploited to produce highly expressive paintings. However, perhaps the most common of all mixtures is the use of marble powder with oils.

Oils can be manipulated by adding granulated materials that alter their texture, and can even be combined on the surface with other painting procedures.

The extraordinary versatility and fast drying time of acrylic paints make them particularly adequate for the incorporation of solid substances. You can produce a sandy, jagged surface by

mixing acrylics or latex with solid substances, such as sand, sawdust or fragments of wood. In the same way, acrylic gel can be used to create a textured surface: it can create a sense of

volume and, once it is dry, it can be repainted with oils without varying the texture that has been applied earlier. Solid substances can either be mixed with oils on the palette (so that it can be added to the color as necessary), or it can be powdered onto a support that has been treated with a layer of latex. Gums, latex and acrylics can be used to prepare a well-textured surface with the advantage of a particularly fast drying time. Once the texture that has been applied to the support is dry, you can start scratching the surface with the end of your brush or scraping at it with a spatula. As you paint, always bear the following in mind: the thicker the texture, the less accurately the paint can be manipulated. Paint with solids in them do not draw such defined or soft lines as oily paints without additives. For this reason, you should not seek too detailed a finish, but should concentrate more on the chromatic harmony of the image and

Fig. 1. **Miravet** *by Grau Carod (artist's private collection). The mixture of marble powder and carpenter's glue or latex produces a thick texture that is rough to the touch and ideal for creating volume in a composition. This technique is particularly popular for landscape painting.*

Fig. 2. **Rocky coast** *by Carlant (artist's private collection). Marble powder can also be combined with acrylics. The most common method involves mixing the powder with the colors directly onto the palette, without using latex because acrylics already contain adhesive components. Carlant did just that when he painted this picture.*

on textural effects.

To conclude what has been said here, we could summarize the basic principles of mixed techniques in two statements. First, you need to know how to choose the right medium to get the effect of relief and to achieve the greatest mutual influence between the two mediums. In other words, you need to avoid layers running into each other, unstable fixing and the combination of incompatible procedures on the same support.

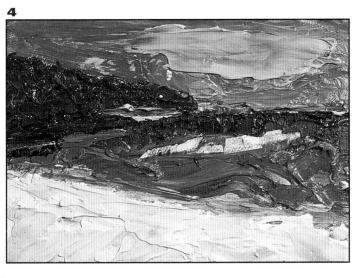

Fig. 3. Pastoral image *by Teresa Trol (artist's private collection). Encaustic painting can produce several attractive effects. Unlike marble powder, it can be used intermittently without the risk of spoiling the film of paint. However, the layer of paint is very sensitive, and the surface should be protected from scraping and scratching.*

Fig. 4. Cuban beach *by Bibiana Crespo (artist's private collection). Medium or thickening gel can add volume to acrylic paints to produce thick, pasty surfaces like this.*

Fig. 5. Arch and palm trees *by Josep Antoni Domingo (artist's private collection). The irregularity and roughness of the wall in the foreground gives the artist the perfect excuse to treat the paint with sawdust to produce a rough, granulated surface. As a result, his strokes seem rather hesitant and confused, which causes the image as a whole to appear somewhat coarse.*

Modeling

This is a procedure in which the material is modeled directly onto the surface of the painting, rather than being mixed into the paint, thus imitating the volume and relief of three-dimensional objects on a flat support. This gives the piece the appearance of a bas-relief. The surface is modeled through the use of cutting, gaps, cracks, and areas of roughness and protrusions that are usually made with a spatula and produce interesting patterns of light and shadow all over the surface of the painting. The most commonly used materials for modeling the surface of the canvas are plaster, pumice stone, marble powder, silicon and papier-mâché, although there are several other less common ones. In general, these materials are incompatible with the actual paint because they tend to alter its characteristics. For example, plaster absorbs oil much too quickly, which means that it cannot be mixed previously on the palette. These substances, with the exception of silicon, are applied directly with a spray gun, and should previously be mixed with carpenter's glue or latex to form a thick paste. The paste is then spread over the support, and the forms of the model are molded with a spatula. You need to shape the surface of the painting into the forms of the model right from the very start. You will not be able to add new pastes or make modifications later on because all of the paste should dry at the same time, and if you add another layer over it, it will not stick properly, and will almost certainly crack.

When the paste that covers the surface of the painting is dry, you can start painting. This way, the material that was used as a texture and your oil or acrylic paints will not be incompatible. This is a wonderful method for creating natural effects and textured landscapes such as rocks and vegetation, but is less appropriate for modeling forms, which requires much more accuracy.

1

Fig. 1. **Es pontas** *by Grau Carod (artist's private collection).* **You can model the forms beforehand with plaster and a spatula. When color is applied to this surface, the different planes will contrast much more strongly.**

2

Fig. 2. **Deep in the wood** *by Grau Carod (artist's private collection).* **The more relief, textures and forms there are in the picture, the more interesting the image will be. This technique provides a wonderful opportunity for modeling new types of form and relief with plaster and thus making the overall effect of a composition more striking.**

3

Fig. 3. Port de la Selva *by Grau Carod (artist's private collection). Working with silicon can be very interesting. Just spray a little silicon onto the palette, add a few drops of thinners and apply the paste you have made to the surface of the painting. The effect is similar to that which you would make with acrylic thickening gels, although silicon tends to be more flexible.*

Fig. 5. Floral composition by Óscar Sanchís (artist's private collection). You can also use silicon for the extracted technique. This involves applying small sprays with a funnel or nozzle. Not only will the the paint seem more voluminous, it will also be more linear.

4

5

Fig. 4. Pallars lake *by Grau Carod (artist's private collection). Silicon pastes tend to produce soft, sinuous effects like the one seen in the foreground of this painting of a lake. You do not need to model too thickly; a subtle texture can often be just as pleasing.*

Pasting with oil paints and a spatula

As we have already suggested, spatula work can be extremely rewarding, and for the amateur artist it is an excellent technique for expressing one's creativity. We are going to observe this by watching how the painter and art teacher, Teresa Trol, tackles the following task. The view shows a village in the Valle de Arán, in the northeast of Spain (fig. 0). This first exercise

Start by painting the sky and the mountains in the background, just thinking about the general color and not about specific details. Notice that Teresa has hardly given any major consideration to the definition of forms. Use different colors to paint the mountainsides and differ-

will be done with oil paints and a spatula. As you can see, the different lines and spatula marks have concentrated on modeling the vegetation, with sharp areas of light and strongly marked contrasts. You should try to imitate the way in which Teresa paints this picture.

Fig. 1. The forms of the landscape are fitted. This first lines should establish the main forms of each plane right from the outset without going into any specific detail. The outline sketch is painted first with a few rough charcoal lines and then with the brush well loaded with dark gray and a touch of thinners. Although you may not think it, when working with pastes, this drawing needs to be well-constructed so that when we come to apply thick layers of color you can base things on your own intuitions. If the outline sketch is not right, you are likely to come across far more problems than you would do normally.

Fig. 2. The first areas of color are painted with a brush and blurred, cloudy colors that have been diluted in plenty of thinners. This allows us to plan the base colors and remove the white of the support from our sight.

ent planes, establishing the different types of terrain.

Fig. 3. At this stage, the early planning of the landscape has been done with very diluted paints and brushes, with only very gently contrasting washes, and with little

MODELS

1-. *The small house* by Karl Schmidt-Rottluff (Thyssen-Bornemisza Museum, Madrid). The use of pastes makes forms much more expressive, but to get the right results you need to understand how to control the direction of your lines. They should outline each form to highlight the voluminous appearance of each element and make the image seem more dynamic.

3

attention given to the outlines and tonal values of each section. Working with such heavily diluted paint means that when you come to use the spatula, it will be used over a layer of very dry thinners, which pasty oil paints stick to particularly well. Having completed this stage, you need to wait for this layer to dry, because otherwise your colors will run along the surface.

Fig. 4. The artist starts on the mountains by mixing masses of violet, emerald green, ochre and white. The pasty and directly painted strokes al-low you to sketch the volumes of the most important features quickly. Notice how the sky has been left in the same color as the original wash. At first, you do not need to fill the picture with too much paint; you can make your colors more pasty as the painting progresses. If you think you have made an area too pasty, you can use your spatula to remove paint while it is still wet. However, to avoid problems later, you should start with a thin background and gradually add thicker layers after.

4

1

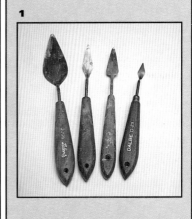

2

Fig. 5. Both the trees and the mountains have been simplified as large areas of color. Although the aim is not make too detailed a representation of the trees, they still look perfectly convincing. The foliage has been painted with directional pastes applied with a short pear-shaped spatula. The earlier

5

greens are covered with pure emerald green and ochre applied with a spatula with its blade held flatly. By adding one color to another in this way, you will see that the mixture produces a special kind of effect. The artist uses the tip of her spatula to practice a little

ula over the same area several times. By repeatedly bringing the spatula into contact with the same area, you will eventually put form into the vegetation. New colors have been added to the leaves of the trees: Naples yellow to the upper section of the foreground

6

graffito on the vegetation in the foreground and thus simulate the directions and forms of the branches.
Fig. 6. Darker colors are now added to give the vegetation its definitive form. To mix the light and dark colors of the vegetation you should move your spat-

and a few touches of red and orange to the lower part of the foreground. The facade of the house is defined with a few touches of color: a little white and ochre for the wall, and burnt umber, sienna and a touch of blue for the shadow cast by the eaves of the roof.

TIPS

3-. If you let thick layers of paint dry slowly, they tend to crack up. To avoid this, use a quick-drying medium or a special mixture for pastes.

4-. If paint is too oily it is difficult to produce pasty strokes. To get around this problem, lay a sheet of newspaper over the paint and leave it there for a few minutes. You will find that the newspaper absorbs the excess oil form the paint and it will now be much more consistent.

3

4

7

8

Fig. 7. Two colors have been used to paint the roof –white and burnt umber. They are applied with the spatula as short, diagonal lines. To finish, the tip of a flexible, steel spatula is used to carefully add a few touches of color, light and texture to specific areas of detail. Contrary to popular opinion, spatula work can be extremely accurate; it all depends on how you hold the spatula when it comes into contact with the surface. It will take a fair amount of practice if you want to perfect the many different techniques, but all kinds of effects and details can be produced. However, one thing should be made clear. You will never be able to achieve the same levels of accuracy with a spatula as you would with brushes.

Fig. 8. The idea of using a spatula with oil paints can be extremely useful when attempting to paint a wide, daring picture like this. If you look carefully at this illustration of the finished painting, you will see a wide variety of different patterns and effects, some of which would be very difficult to produce with a traditional set of brushes. If you try copying this picture, you will probably find that, at least at first, painting with a spatula is much harder than using a brush, and you will need a lot of practice before you are comfortable with the technique.

MODELS

2-. *Autumn sea XI* by Emil Nolde (Kunsthaus, Zurich). This painting by Nolde expresses different atmospheric conditions through the use of pastes and carefully controlled directional lines. The long, horizontal lines that are used for the coastline, and the more scribbled, vertical ones that are used for the sky and clouds add a strong sense of emotion to the painting.

2

Pasting with acrylics and a medium

In this exercise the painter and illustrator Josep Antoni Domingo, an expert landscapist, is going to paint a landscape using acrylics and a medium, alternating between spatulas and brushes as the painting progresses.

You can paint any subject you like with a spatula, but you will generally get the best results if you paint subjects that don't require too much detail, as is the case with this view of a village in the Catalan Pyrenees in Spain (fig. 0).

2

To do this exercise, the artist has mixed acrylic paints with a gel type medium (made up of a cellulose thickener) which helps to spread the color and give it more volume. Learning to use a spatula is no easy task, but if you practice enough you

1

0

will soon find that they can be used for as many different purposes as you could use a brush for.

Fig. 1. As is common practice when painting a landscape, the artist starts with the sky. There are two reasons for doing this. Firstly, the color of the sky determines every other color in a landscape, and secondly it is usually the part with less texture and is therefore smoother. Notice that the color is

applied directly, with no preparatory sketch. Mix cobalt blue and white in different proportions to represent the irregular tones and forms of the clouds. It is a good idea to hold the spatula flatly and move it along the surface so that the colors run smoothly. Try mixing the colors directly onto the support and superimpose your spatula marks. Notice that the artist leaves a few small areas of white that will help define the clouds. As he paints the sky, he also sketches the

MODELS

1

1-. *Sorrow* by Jack Yeats (National Gallery of Ireland). Over a background of diluted colors, the artist has applied a serious of vigorous pastes that turn a figurative urban scene into one that is almost abstract. Pasting allows you to build up a painting with areas of imprecise color that, rather than having a detailed finish, concentrate more on the strength and expressiveness of pastes.

3

ken colors. Do not worry about using too much gel or medium –the more you add to your paint, the greater sense of volume it will produce.

Fig. 3. The artist continues modeling the surface of the painting. Once he has completed the upper section of the, he starts coloring the area below that corresponds to the field in the foreground. He uses four basic colors for the task –cadmium yellow, ochre, and small touches of green and burnt umber.

With a flat spatula he superimposes colors and scrapes a few areas with its edge to produce the contrast between masses of color and the areas where the white of the support can still be seen.

mountain slope with an intense and somewhat more uniform violet.

Fig. 2. Keep working on the sky and add a little more white to the clouds. The different tones that the artist uses for the meadow in the center of the picture can be painted with combinations of dark cadmium green, cadmium yellow and touches of ochre.

The different textures are produced by horizontally and vertically dragging one color over another, taking care not to press too hard or take color away with the edge of your spatula. The surface color should include irregular pastes that produce chromatic variations and bro-

4

TIPS

1-. Flat and synthetic brushes are the best ones for working with pastes because they are able to hold more paint.

2.- Never apply more than about five centimeters of paint, or that on the outside will dry much quicker than that on the inside and the surface will crack.

1

2

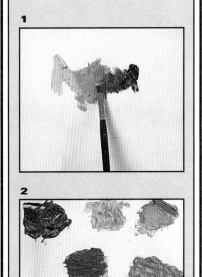

This involves working on the impact of colors, leaving some areas white and applying areas of color with the spatula held at a slant, lifting it up and down to recreate the idea of roughness.

Fig. 4. With a small, flat brush, he starts painting the village. He uses a range of ochres, siennas and pinks to paint the uniform colors of the walls of the houses. To paint the colors of the path, you can use some of the colors you used earlier: ochre, yellow and light green, but now make them

5

much pastier. You should not let these colors blend into each other. Applying different amounts of pressure will make the textures much more evocative. Now add a few touches of burnt umber to the cornfield in the foreground to define that part of the picture a little more. To accentuate the

difference between the planes of the picture even more clearly, add a large amount of paint and more intense colors to the edges of the different fields, thus defining the borders between each area of color.

Fig. 5. Using the same brush, you should now work on the mountains. You should use more violet and pink tones due to the rule of interposed atmosphere (as you should already know, the more distant planes of an image always look grayer and less colorful). So, the mountains should look rather grayish. Use similar gray tones for the parts of the buildings in the shadow and for the roofs of the village. Spend a few minutes looking over what you have done up until now, and work out where you still need to work on the color. Use a spatula to add a mixture of white and ochre to a few parts of the foreground, then go back to work with your brushes.

Fig. 6. Use a brush to start adding more accurate touches of color than those that you applied with spatulas.

6

TIPS

3-. Remember that thick paint tends to stand out in a painting, so if you want to keep a sense of depth and perspective in the image, you should only use it for the foreground and/or the most important features.

4-. When using oil paints, another popular technique involves applying veils on top of pastes. However, it is quicker and easier to use acrylics for this because they dry so much faster.

3

4

With a brush, it is easier to produce more precise patterns and gestures. A few strokes of white and emerald green will brighten up the meadow. Your stokes need to be synthetic and

7

8

something which is particularly true of landscape paintings. The freely pasted surface of the painting comes from the use of paint mixed with a thickening medium. One last point –when you paint pictures like this, the paint should always be malleable, but at the same time thick enough to conserve the lines and strokes that were made by the spatula.

should never mix with the colors underneath. You should use similar strokes to work on the flat, uniform colors of the houses in the village.

Fig. 7. With a thin brush, add detail to the doors and windows, paint the roofs with shades of red and draw thin, solid lines to suggest the outlines of some of the buildings. The artist has spread a few areas of turquoise blue (made by mixing emerald green and touches of white and blue) over the surface of the fields in the middle ground. These are painted in a pointillist way, which is a useful method for interpreting the texture of grass, and such variety of texture helps to make the picture more interesting. Put brown onto a spatula and add a little contrast to the foreground.

Fig. 8. The end result of this exercise includes a wide variety of evocative textures, and shows just what can be done when a spatula is used properly. The finished picture is full of expressiveness, reinforced by the pasty colors and the marks made by the spatula. Notice how descriptive the synthesis is when created with a spatula,

MODELS

2-. *Tugboat on the Elbe* by Emil Nolde (private collection, Hamburg). The rough surface of the water and the cloudy, yellowish sky are perfectly recaptured by the moving nature of the spatula lines that the artist has used. The forms are never still, they flow constantly. This is typical of the kind of modern, contemporary painting that has turned Nolde into one of the outstanding painters of the postimpressionist era.

2

Painting on glass: Sgraffito

The artist Óscar Sanchís, who has already proved his worth in other books in this collection, is going to show us how to use sgraffito on a glass surface. The subject is this pretty composition showing a windmill, a small waterfall and hundred of leafless branches in the foreground (fig. 0). There are several advantages to this exercise, firstly, the artist can explore the many variations on the original design, color and texture and secondly he will be working on a repellent surface (one that does not absorb any paint), making his brushstrokes flow more smoothly. You will find just how fascinating, yet at the same time

challenging, sgraffito can be. To do this exercise, all you need is a sheet of glass, normal oil painting materials and a rubber tipped brush.

Fig. 1. Clean the glass and put it over a sheet of white paper that will serve as your background and help to visualize each color as it is applied. The next step involves coloring the glass base as freely as you like, adding a uniform ochre to the area where the building stands and a few areas of burnt umber and gray over the vegetation. You can use more than one color for this. These colors should be thick and should not contain too much thinners or else they would run all over the smooth surface of the glass. If you do want to dilute any of your colors, you would be better off using a little medium.

Fig. 2. The top of the picture is painted with a flat brush. Notice how the bristles leave their grooved forms on the surface of the glass. Because glass does not absorb any paint at all, you should take an awful lot of care not to let any new colors you add mix into those below. Paint alla prima, applying the

local color of each area right from the very start, thus avoiding the need to go over the same area any more than is absolutely necessary. If you were to work in separate sessions, waiting for each new layer to dry before carrying on, you would not be able to use the

MODELS

1-. *Street market* by Óscar Sanchís (artist's private collection). Color applied directly onto glass stays fluid and fresh. Strokes tend to contain grooves and two or three colors together tend to dirty each other. This painting looks a bit like the kind of outdoor sketches that are usually painted *alla prima*.

3

sgraffito technique, which always requires the paint to be wet.

Fig. 3. We are still at the initial stage, now using thicker and denser paint. Notice how the ochre of the windmill is now more opaque and compact, whereas the color of the waterfall is much more fluid. Along the edges of the river the strokes look like rough scribbles (the strokes are imitating the turbulent nature of the water, and thus help to portray the sensation of movement). Ochres, earth colors, blues and siennas are juxtaposed onto each other to create dirtier shades. This is a comfortable way of working because, if you do not like the way that things have turned out, it is easy to just clean the glass and start all over again.

Fig. 4. Now paint

the darker areas with burnt umber, ultramarine blue and sienna. Although these strokes are denser and applied more carefully, the paint is still not equal because glass has no pores and its texture does not retain any of the particles of pigment. If you need to paint lines on glass, you should paint them over a pre-painted background. To draw these lines, the paint should be a bit more diluted than before, but still full of plenty of pigment. Draw these lines slowly, because if you do not the strokes will end up looking too light. The artist has done this to draw the lines of branches that appear in the foreground.

Fig. 5. If you need a degraded or uniform tone, you will need to manipulate paint after you have applied it. Your fingers are often better than any

4

TIPS

1-. If you insist on working over an outline sketch, you can do this on the white paper that is put under the glass at the start of the exercise. This paper will serve as a guide when you apply the first layers of paint.

2-. When painting on glass you can make as many modifications and corrections as you like, you just have to wipe the paint off with a clean cloth.

1

2

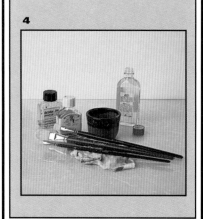
5

artificial tool, and you can produce areas of tone and texture simply by rubbing the paint with your fingertips. But you should be extremely careful not to accidentally touch the painting with any other part of your body, because any contact will immediately leave its mark, and could ruin all your good work. But it is probably the best way of producing medium tones and degradations.

Fig. 6. Now you need to work a little on details before starting the sgraffito process. With a medium brush, the artist applies a few small, thick stokes of white to the waterfall, which is combined with sky blue and violet reflections. Color the lights of the windmill with tenuous shades of yellow. Paint the bottom of the painting with cadmium green and blend that color into

those that surround it. Paint over the ochre facade with burnt umber to suggest the openings in the building. Notice how, as the painting develops, the paint is getting thicker and thicker. This is absolutely crucial when painting with the sgraffito technique.

Fig. 7. Now that the layer of paint is thicker, you can start scraping and carving into the surface with the rubber tipped brush. While the paint is still wet, press the rubber tip onto the surface of the glass to start drawing the patterns of vegetation in the foreground. This is ideal for defining outlines and expressive details. If you copy what the artist is doing, you will soon realize just how flexible sgraffito work on glass can be, and the amazing versatility of a rubber tipped brush depending on the amount of pressure that you apply. You can use all kinds of different objects for sgraffito: pins, nails, spatulas, screwdrivers, coins, brushes or even your own fingernails.

Fig. 8. Notice what unique lines the

6

rubber tipped brush has produced, and how textured the surface is when using this rich technique. If there is any contrast between the colors and tones of the film of wet paint and the color beneath, the borders are clearly highlighted. It is as well-defined as a print and has the sensitivity of a traditional line drawing but manages to transmit a unique lively sensation. Once

8

the painting is dry, rather than framing it conventionally, you might prefer to use a box of light (placing a diffused light just behind the glass). This will make the sgraffito effects stand out even more.

MODELS

2

2-. *House in the mountains* by Óscar Sanchís (artist's private collection). Pictures like this, painted on glass or plastic, combine the use of color pastes and sgraffito in the same piece. Sgraffito is the most appropriate of the two methods for describing the leafless branches that appear in this picture. Because glass does not absorb the oil out of paint, the colors seem brighter and glossier, as if the linseed oil had dried into a layer of varnish over the surface of the paint.

A tissue paper collage

Moving on from pasting techniques, we shall now look at collages, the technique that involves sticking things onto a support. The painter and sculptor, Carlant, is going to show us how to make a relief collage using tissue paper (preferably sticking the paper to the support with latex). The composition can either be made up of forms that are carefully cut out or loosely torn, and then sculpted by folding or wrinkling the tissue to make the kinds of relief and

1

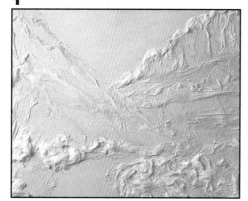

0

2

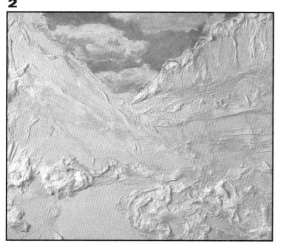

texture that will make the surface of the picture more interesting. These increase the expressiveness and tactile qualities of the image. This collage is going to be based on this photograph of a mountain pass in the Moroccan desert. (fig. 0).

Fig. 1. Using the photograph as a guide, the artist starts sticking the wrinkled tissue paper to the surface of the support with latex as he molds the forms of the mountains and the rocks

along the edge of the path. The idea is to apply strips of paper so that they imitate the shapes of the cracks and streaks in the rocky mountains. The slopes in the foreground are the most pronounced forms, while no collage is used for the sky at all, which is left completely flat to help accentuate the sense of depth in the landscape. What will make your collage a good one is not the quality of the materials you use but the way in which you use them. Whether the artist is an amateur or a professional, tissue paper can produce extremely satisfactory results,

Fig. 2. Once you have stuck the pieces of paper in their places, you already have the basic structure that you need

MODELS

1

1-. *The Sphinx* by Josep Antoni Domingo (artist's private collection). Any part of a landscape with a certain amount of volume and texture can be represented with crumpled tissue paper. But the paper should be folded carefully and should follow the same rhythms as the model itself, in this case the rocky structure of the Sphinx and the voluptuous forms of the clouds.

3

for painting. Nevertheless, you should wait a day for the glue to dry before continuing. It is probably best to start with the sky, using ultramarine blue nearer to the top and adding more sky blue as you move downwards. In doing this, you are applying the first layer of color to the whole area that makes up

which helps to suggest volume. You can add a little Naples yellow to this gray to break the monotony.

Fig. 3. The upper section has now been colored, and so the artist moves downwards and starts defining the different parts of the mountainsides. The artist paints the interesting rhythms of tone and color that appear in the rocks, dirtying violets and greens with earthy colors for the mountain on the right and using sienna and burnt umber for the one on the left. It's almost impossible to paint a uniform wash over crumpled up tissue paper because there are always going to be a few parts that

4

the upper section of the painting. Notice how the tops of the clouds are of the same color as the white of the support, but lower down they are grayer,

don't get colored and which the bristles of your brush can sometimes only reach after quite a lot of effort. Instead of trying to get rid of all these white spaces,

TIPS

1-. One important consideration when we use paper as the material for a collage is the fact that its edges will react to paint in a very different way depending on whether you cut it or tear it. Frayed, torn edges can be much more suggestive and expressive.

2-. Dry strokes can produce much better results than veils when applied to a surface with a texture like the one in this exercise. If you work in this way, paint will accumulate on the folds and wrinkles that the paper forms.

1

2

5

perhaps it would be better to leave them as they are because they add a certain textural variety to the piece.

Fig. 4. With a flat brush and new layers of color, the artist carries on filling in the white areas of the picture. He blends his colors, forming soft grada-

6

tions on the surface of the painting. A good example of this is the hill on the left with its gradations of green and dark gray. Rather than being uniform, the color is modified by the white spaces that are caused by the wrinkles in the paper. This way of working from

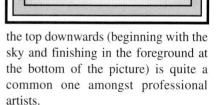
the top downwards (beginning with the sky and finishing in the foreground at the bottom of the picture) is quite a common one amongst professional artists.

Fig. 5. All of the general values have been completed, and now it is time to paint the stony path in the foreground. Once the basic structure has been established you can start thinking about details. You may have noticed that we have not used any shadows up until now, and so, before he colors any more of the painting, Carlant starts adding

7

strokes with different bright blue, red and ochre tones in the central section. He insinuates the stones with small touches of his brush, bringing purer colors and tones into the picture that blend into the more neutral ones in the background. The great advantage of this art form is that you can experiment with the paper as much as you like before you actually stick it to the surface of the picture. You can then paint on dry to make the effect stronger and the wrinkled forms of the paper are highlighted even more by the way that paint accumulates on the jagged edges.

contrast to the middle ground, which puts more depth and volume into the composition. With a spatula and raw umber he casts the shadows of the most prominent rocks on the left-hand mountain and the rocky area in the bottom right hand corner. With the same spatula, but this time with an intense ultramarine blue, he paints the cracks and the dark base of the right hand peak. Then he loads his brush with black paint and adds a few touches to the lower section of the picture, just above the path.

Fig. 6. The best part of the shading is now complete. Over the medium intensity tones, start painting a progressive series of contrasts that outline the most relevant areas. You can add more details to the lower section of the painting using darker and more concise lines. The path still looks rather sketchy, almost impressionist, but can be touched up with neutral colors like gray, brown, ochre and a few bluish tones. Take care over the texture of your strokes; you should use short, pasty lines. As you can see, a few ochres, whites and grays have been mixed directly on the surface of the painting.

Fig. 7. To compensate the tones in the foreground, Carlant applies short

MODELS

2-. *Montserrat* by Grau Carod (artist's private collection). Shapes formed with tissue paper can be of whatever size and as wrinkled as we like. Just remember that the more tissue you use, the less detail you will be able to be paint later. You may find that it is better to leave your painting in a sketchy or embryonic state, which does not necessarily mean it does not look interesting.

2

Still life with pieces of cloth

For this exercise, the artist Sofía Isus has made a collage using different cuttings of cloth, some strips have patterns on them, others are checked and others are plain. She also uses a variety of different textures. The chosen model needs to be simple, with clear and well-defined forms. A still life is an ideal subject (like the one that we have chosen for this step-by-step exercise, with a jug and a bowl of fruit). The idea is to break it down into different planes of light and color, but still maintaining a varied array of attractive forms. Let your imagination run freely as it plays with the richness of color and texture, but never stop concentrating on the shapes of the objects. This is not a difficult exercise provided you follow what the artist does carefully.

The nice thing about this kind of exercise is that you can try out all kinds of different ideas before you decide on the definitive collage.

Fig. 2. Once you have decided which colors and patterns you are going to use in your

design, stick them in the right places and start painting. With a large brush, apply the first colors: cobalt blue and

Fig. 1. Study the model carefully. When making a collage, you should not aim to reproduce every detail perfectly, but to summarize the main elements. Using strips of cloth with different colors and patterns, construct each of the main features. You do not necessarily have to limit yourself to what you see in real life – this is an exercise in creativity and should only be an interpretation of reality.

MODELS

1-. *In the market* by Óscar Sanchís (artist's private collection). Working with strips of cloth can be an interesting exercise, and can produce attractive results. The different types of material add chromatic variety to the piece, something that is harder to do using paints, and the combination of shapes and pattern creates a unique graphic richness. You do not usually need to use much paint, because a good collage should be able to work well enough on its own.

3

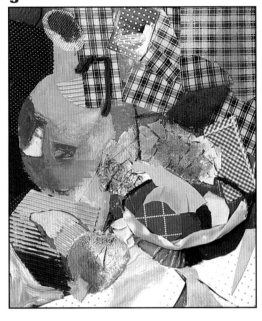

a little white to indicate, with expressive, vigorous strokes, the volume of the jar. Then, using the on dry technique and a little yellow and orange, paint the first layers of color on the apple and the melon. This does not mean that you should cover everything that you have done up until now with paint, but rather that you should find ways of complementing it. You should try to combine the colors and patterns on the pieces of cloth with new strokes that help to describe the forms of the objects, contrasts and touches of light better.

Fig. 3. The series of new colors not only brings more life to the composition, but also makes the overall structure more acceptable. The artist adds a gray wash to the lower section of the jug; adds green to the melon; burnt umber to the curved structure of the carton (in the bottom left); uses a medium rounded brush loaded with black to define the outline of the fruit bowl and finally, with a light violet, she spreads opaque

washes over the lower section of the painting to indicate areas of shadow and the folds in the table cloth. You will notice that the paint does not always stick very well onto the occasionally rather porous surface of the pieces of cloth. To get over this problem, use pastier colors or use a gel or medium to make the color more consistent.

4

Fig. 4. Add a few expressive and textural details to the picture by applying paint either with your brush or a spatula. You need to contrast the forms even more so that they stand out against the background. To do this, the artist has used indigo and claret for the left outline of the jug, and has used the same colors to define the form of the melon and the edge of the apple next to the lemon in the foreground; with titanium white she colors the edge of the neck and handle of the jug so that its silhouette is clearer. Finally, she applies a

TIPS

1-. You should use a strong, white sheet of card as your base, because it will not spoil so easily and the white color will help make each of the pieces of material stand out more clearly.

2-. One usually starts by planning the design. If you like, make a preparatory sketch on the support (in diagrammatic form), although if you prefer, you can skip this stage and start work with the picture itself.

1

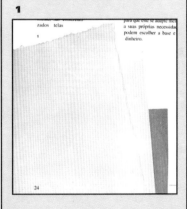

2

5

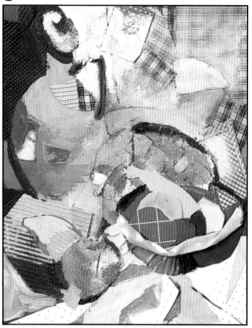

few patches of yellow, pink and violet to the central section and uses a little ochre for the shadows on the cloth at the bottom of the picture.

Fig. 5. With colors with a certain pastel tendency, the artist covers the upper right hand section, reducing the effect of the pattern of squares. The pattern should not be hidden com-

6

pletely because it is quite interesting; a few medium intensity washes should suffice. By making the background brighter, the foreground gains in importance and the objects that make up the still life stand out more.

Fig. 6. Once the main structure has been established, the artist can start thinking about details. Not happy with the form of the melon, she decides to cover it with pieces of card and colored paper that she has cut with a pair of scissors. Having rectified the error, she paints the melon with opaque, grooved strokes using unequal proportions of cadmium red, ochre and white. She paints the banana in a similar way using cadmium yellow and black. The artist uses a wide range of pastes and varies her technique as she applies paint to the support, with an aim to create the dimensions of the textures of the finished painting.

Fig. 7. The flexibility of this procedure allows you to create a convincing sense of space and structure if

you use cutout shapes for the areas o shadow and light. Notice such shape on the outline of the jug, where the artist has used small red strips t highlight the as yet poorly define outline of the jug. The outline no looks less broken and has a more de liberate finish. It does not take long t

7

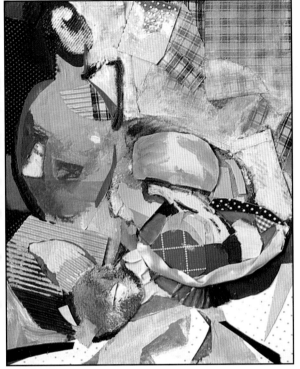

8

make a collage like this, and before you know it, you will be applying the finishing touches.

Fig. 8. This exercise combines two techniques: painting and collage. The end result is not just a convincing representation of the objects, but is also a pleasant, decorative image. The pieces of cloth combine nicely with the painted areas to create an attractive surface. There is almost a sense of movement in the image, caused by the harmony and disharmony between the colors and effects. Some colors stand out, while others fade into the background, and similarly colored areas relate to each other and move the spectator's eyes across the surface of the painting.

MODELS 2

2-. *The Liceo theater* by Gabriel Martín (artist's private collection). A collage made with pieces of cloths produces an interesting array of wrinkles on the surface of the support and can create abstract impressions like this one. Although it is clearly a picture of an opera theater, the style is much closer to being Informalist than figurative.

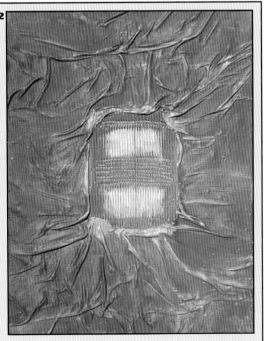

Textures with organic elements

All of the exercises that we have been doing up until now have made use of very traditional materials, albeit in unusual ways. For the next exercise, the painter and etcher, Bibiana Crespo, is going to combine the use of

paint with organic elements stuck to a rigid support. The subject she has chosen is this view of a hermitage over a wall of rock (fig. 0). After studying the subject, she gathers a selection of materials that she feels are the right ones to add to the surface of her picture. Let's see what she does with them.

Fig. 1. Once she has found the right

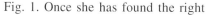

subject, she gathers the different materials: leaves, twigs, vegetables, sand, soil, pasta and glue, as well as a pair of scissors and an appropriate support. She then draws a simple sketch onto the support and slowly and carefully sticks the different objects onto it. She starts with the larger objects and then adds smaller materials. She has used latex glue to stick everything to the surface.

Fig. 2. You should always let the glue dry for a few hours, or even a whole day if you have the patience. When it is dry at last, the artist takes a rounded brush with synthetic bristles (because they are more resistant to working on textured surfaces) and colors the walls of the hermitage with plenty of beige and sienna paint. The openings are painted with burnt umber on the walls and ultramarine blue for the chapel and the apse. With a medium intensity gray, she paints the shadow of the bell tower on the roof.

Fig. 3. The grains of rice that simulate the stones that hold the building up are painted with an ochre that has been lightened with white. Be generous with the paint you use, it should be pasty rather than diluted. With the same ochre, but now dirtied with a little sienna, paint the bell tower. Paint its roof with burnt umber. You should deal with the larger areas of color first and then move on to details, although you can't be too fancy

MODELS

1-. *The wood*, by Grau Carod (artist's private collection). Sticking organic elements onto a surface can often make it very hard to paint. So this technique is probably most valid for sketchy, expressionist ideas with little attention to detail.

3

when making this sort of picture.

Fig. 4. Now that the main architectonic elements of the hermitage have been established, the artist starts painting the background. Start with the craggy mountainsides using unequal and diffused shades of permanent green and continue with a little ochre in the lighter areas and emerald green and raw umber for the shadowed parts. Imagine that you are constructing a stage set, with a bright foreground contrast-

ed against a darker backdrop. For this reason, the artist has lightened the color of the roof and bell tower of the hermitage.

Fig. 5. In this illustration, you can clearly see the way that the artist has used different materials to create a variety of textures. The rough, irregular surface that these materials create makes it difficult to paint many details, obliging you to paint a rough, impressionist image. So, the artist

4

thinks about the image as a whole and takes the maximum advantage of the patterns of light and shadow that the textures and materials stuck to the support offer.

Fig. 6. The painting is finished. Look at the use of ochres, pinks and siennas mixed with plenty of white to brighten the foreground,. The silhouette of the hermitage stands out clear-

5

ly against the duller background, which has been dyed with grays, dirtied greens and umbers. The bright colors in the foreground reappear in the top right hand section of the picture, although they are more diluted to give the impression of distance. The painting as a whole, although it is not particularly detailed, captures the atmosphere of the place very well and offers an interesting study of light and shadow.

6

Everyday objects

Collage work is not limited to just flat or two-dimensional objects. Many artists have been able to produce passionate, creative images with three-dimensional objects that are

2

with a little latex.

Fig. 2. Once the objects are stuck on the support, we place the board upright and start painting them. The artist begins

1

by turning the floppy disc into a jug, and uses raw umber to outline the table. The piece of paper on the right is painted in the dark olive green color of a bottle. With a few quick strokes, the compact disc becomes a coffee cup complete with saucer. To paint, the artist only uses a couple of tones of each color, a light one for the lit areas and a dark one to indicate shadow. Notice the interesting relationship between the painted cup and the real teaspoon.

transformed into fascinating pictures. In this next exercise, Bibiana Crespo is going to do just that –she will use everyday objects to compose a still life, and then finish off her work with the use of oil paints. This is a very different way of approaching a subject, yet it is an unusual context that produces a fresh way of seeing things.

Fig. 1. As you can well imagine, there is no preparatory sketch. The composition is established by playing around with the objects and trying them out in different positions on the support until the result looks satisfactory. However, as you will see, the artist continues adding new objects to the composition as she paints, changing the appearance of the picture significantly. Once the chosen objects have been placed on the support –a floppy disc, a plastic cup, a compact disc, a piece of a serviette, a teaspoon, adhesive tape, buttons and some pills with their plastic cases– the artist starts sticking them down

MODELS

1-. *Window* by Teresa Trol (artist's private collection). Here is an interesting visual pattern; the artist has stuck a wooden frame onto the support to form a window, and this three dimensional object plays an active role in the landscape. The combination of flat and shaped objects confuses the spectator. The composition suggests that art can act as a window on the world.

1

3

Fig. 3. The artist keeps adding new strokes to the picture. She paints the shadow of the bottle with the same dirtied green that she used for the object itself. With a medium intensity gray, she colors the background with an attractive geometric design. She pauses for a while, and studies her work to make sure that the objects are all p r o p e r l y shaped. She says that she is not happy with what she sees, and decides to add new materials to modify or complement those that she has used up until now. However, she will not be doing this until this preparatory stage has been completed.

Fig. 4. To give more volume to the plastic cup, she paints its shape with a gray that is dirtied with green, as if

4

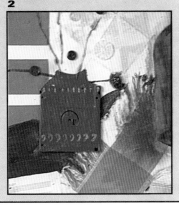
it was made of glass. With pink strokes for the transparent parts and with white to simulate reflections, the cup takes on its final appearance. Using burnt umber and a touch of gray, she casts the shadow of the cup across the tablecloth. All of these effects aim to improve the sense of

3

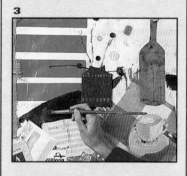

4

5

volume of each individual object and also of the image as a whole.

Fig. 5. As our work progresses, we find new and more creative ways of approaching the subject. This sometimes implies being somewhat more destructive and removing certain objects, and some parts of the picture need to be transformed completely to give them whole new meanings. The artist has cut out a piece of porexpan to represent the jug; a cardboard kitchen roll and a piece of wood for the bottle and pieces of plastic, candy wrappers and clothes pegs for the shape of the flowers. Once these new materials have been formed, the artist carefully sticks them onto the picture with latex.

Fig. 6. When the latex is dry and the materials are firmly stuck, we can start painting again. Start by painting the jug with a combination of ochre, burnt umber and touches of blue and white. She has continued working on the flowers at the top with new and dirtier washes that will act as a background to the new, brighter colors that will represent the brightness and form of the flowers. This section still isn't finished, and the artist needs to add new materials to the flowers to give them a better sense of volume.

6

7

Fig. 7. She works on the painting as a whole, and as each of the elements now looks more voluminous, she needs to work on the flat areas of the composition so that they relate coherently to the rest of the picture. To do this, the artist works even more on the contrasts of light and shadow on the cup by adding ultramarine blue at the top and by applying washes at its base to cast its shadow. Notice how other elements of the picture, such as the teaspoon and even the tiny pills also have cleverly painted shadows. With a mixture of cobalt blue and

permanent green, she paints the cylindrical surface of the bottle. The way in which this bottle has been painted might remind you of some of Picasso's paintings.

Fig. 8. The artist has added new materials for the flowers: buttons, cartons, cigarette ends and pieces of sponge. As soon as they are dry she paints them with bright colors, although these stokes are quite rough and lack detail. Just as she did with the other objects, she has cast the shadow, albeit somewhat more

8

lightly, on the left of the jug. After studying her work for a few minutes, and applying a few finishing touches here and there, she decides the painting is finished. The objects that have been selected and stuck to the support may at first seem rather trivial, but they have been positioned so skillfully onto the support that the final effect is quite impressive.

MODELS 2

2-. *Still life of a clock and a jar with flowers* by Grau Carod (artist's private collection). The success of this exercise depends entirely on the creativity of the artist. The idea is to collect waste materials, study them for a while and try to work out where to put them in the composition and what new objects they can represent. The results might not be overly picturesque, but it is a good exercise in developing your creativity.

View of Venice with marble powder

1

0

In this next exercise we are going to see how the painter Grau Carod paints a view of Venice from the tower of Saint Mark's Basilica (fig. 0), creating textures with latex and marble powder. For this mixed media technique, you will need to use a thick medium such as oil paint, perhaps mixed with a more acrylic procedure such as latex.

Fig. 1. First pour 250 grams of latex and 200 grams of marble powder into a bowl, add a little water and stir the mixture until you have made a consistent, easily manipulated paste. Study the model and start molding the surface of the board with a spatula. Try to represent the model

using pastes at different intervals so that the white of the support shows through between the different pastes. You will notice that the paste looks gray when it is still white, but it will lightly whiten as it dries. Your support needs to be flat when you are applying marble powder.

Fig. 2. Once the surface has hardened, you can start painting, just as you would do on any other kind of support. Start with the sky and the horizon using different gradations of cobalt blue, and then color the base of the domes of St Mark's Basilica with orange and sienna. With a little carmine and a touch of white and ochre, roughly sketch the rooftop landscape in the background. You should not work in sections, you should always be thinking about the image as a whole, and work on every section at the same time. These first colors should be diluted in thinners so that the paint flows more easily on such a textured surface.

Fig. 3. The artist adds ochre, lightened with white, to the colors that were originally applied to the dome and roofs of the basilica. For the facade (in the bottom, right hand section), use the

MODELS

1-. *Landscape*, by Ester Llaudet (artist's private collection). Marble powdered surfaces, despite their austerity and hardness, are notably colorful and textural. The combination of oil paints and marble powder is one of the most popular mixed techniques of the modern day.

1

2

stage is complete, the image is still looking quite sketchy.

Fig. 4. At this early stage of the color plan, the artist uses thick, deliberate strokes to avoid having to add too much detail. This is a useful tactic for designing a wide, daring composition. As you can see from this blown up image, both the roofs and the domes have been simplified into large areas of simple colors, and

3

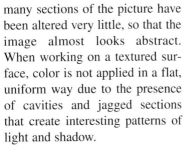

same ochre but this time a little purer. Use ivory black strokes to draw the lines that clarify the different sections of the roof, and then use a grayish wash that has been heavily diluted with thinners to color the bottom right hand section of the painting. Starting with just three or four colors, the artist establishes the base of the composition and the general color code. When this

4

many sections of the picture have been altered very little, so that the image almost looks abstract. When working on a textured surface, color is not applied in a flat, uniform way due to the presence of cavities and jagged sections that create interesting patterns of light and shadow.

Fig. 5. The main tonal values of the piece have been established, although they are not necessarily going to be the definitive colors. There is a considerable amount of alteration to be done, but the support needs to be covered along with the grayish marble powder

TIPS

1-. By mixing latex with marble powder we get a pasty solution (similar to cement) that can be applied to canvas to create textures and relief.

2-. When working on a textured marble powder surface you need to use resistant brushes, such as horsehair ones. If you use softer brushes, you will be shocked at how quickly they deteriorate. Brushes wear away due to the erosive action produced by rubbing against the rough, granulated surface of the marble powder.

1

2

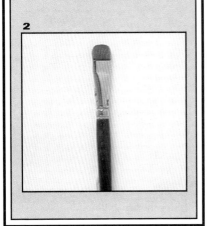

paste. However, the focal points of the painting, the domes of the basilica and the main areas of light and shadow, are

6

already complete. The background is full of roofs, painted with successive and superimposed layers of orange, ochre, earth and a touch of gray (which is reflected in the clouds and in the bell tower in the distance).

Fig. 6. The lower part of the painting is now developed with areas of color that merge together at the edges. The overlaps and pinnacles at the sides are painted with blue where there is shadow and Naples yellow where sunlight is shining. On the pinnacles at the top of the facade there is more burnt umber in the mixtures of color. After these initial studies, which have basically used paint diluted in thinners, the artist starts using denser, thicker paint. From now on, you should blend your colors more, applying paint with a gentle, rubbing movement so

5

that color is deposited on the edges and lumps in the paste to produce a better sense of relief.

Fig. 7. We can now see a few architectonic details such as the windows, the molded dome, lanterns, overlaps and pinnacles. Trying to put more detail into the buildings would be a mistake, because you can't be too fancy when working on such a rough texture. As he goes on, the artist adds a few linear

MODELS

2

2-. *Between the branches*, by Grau Carod (artist's private collection). The control of strokes and a paste made with marble powder help create a sense of relief and depth in the paint. There are different types of marble powder, from very smooth powders, where the particles are so small that they are practically undetectable, to those that feel like sand and produce much rougher, more granulated surfaces.

7

references with a small brush. Such references are useful for clarifying the image, and if they did not exist, it would looked rather blurry and unfocussed.

Fig. 8. By leaving the bottom of the picture so sketchy, just painted with a few imprecise, unfocussed strokes, the image is projected vertically and majestically accentuates the domes in the center of the image. This is a common trick in photography and given that, since Impressionism began, painting has adopted several photographic effects, it is also a common technique in modern day landscapes. This blurred and imprecise finish suggests movement and the fleeting qualities of light, always changing in both urban and rural landscapes.

8

Flowers with latex and sawdust

We continue with Grau Carod, and some new experiments with mixed techniques. In this exercise, our base will be made up of latex and sawdust to create a textured surface that we shall then paint with oil paints. The subject is this simple vase of flowers (fig. 0). Flowers are a highly appropriate theme for material paintings because they do not need too much planning and neither does the finish have to be too elaborate.

Fig. 1. First, you should prepare the mixture of latex and sawdust. To create the sandy texture, you should use more sawdust than latex. If the mixture is too dense, add a little water to

make it more fluid. Once the mixture is ready, start spreading it over the surface with a spatula. Notice that the artist has not tried to even out the lumps formed by the sawdust so as to make his surface as textured as possible. To create a variety of textures, leave some spaces blank and in others apply greater proportions of latex than sawdust. Open spaces in the sawdust

with the end of your spatula or a fingernail.

Fig. 2. When the mixture is dry, start applying color. Remember that any paste made with sawdust will take longer to dry than a marble powder one because damp sawdust absorbs water and holds it for longer. So you should wait a couple of days before continuing. Then, take a number eight

brush and add the first touches to the flowers, mixing cadmium red and carmine. You should put plenty of paint on your brush and press the bristles into the cavities in the granulated paste.

Fig. 3. Keep planning the form of the flowers with imprecise ochre and burnt umber strokes mixed with a little green. Add a little white to cobalt blue in varying proportions on the surface of the vase. Position the areas of light and shadow from the start,

MODELS

1-. *Rural landscape*, by Óscar Sanchís (artist's private collection). This painting was made using the on dry technique. Starting with a support covered with latex and sawdust means that paint accumulates on the bumps and points that the materials create on the surface. The resulting strokes are broken and granulated. This can clearly be seen in the floor in the foreground.

3

helping to mold the volume of the model before moving onto more intense colors. To make the background coherent, the artist spreads a wide latex wash. While the support is still wet, sprinkle sand over the whole of the surface of the background so that the texture relates better to that of the vase, because otherwise these two areas would contrast excessively.

Fig. 4. Dye the background with pink, using paint that has been well diluted in thinners to form a degradation (more intense at the top and getting lighter as you

6

move down the picture). Use successive strokes as you put more volume into the bunch of flowers. Place spots of white into the illuminated area to the right and darken the left with cobalt blue, something which will help to define the contours of the vase. Paint the vase by adding carmine to the cobalt blue you used before, thus creating a violet tone that harmonizes with the carmine color of the flowers and the pink in the background. With a little black, paint the three iron stanchions that hold the vase.

Fig. 5. The artist adds new shades of color to the flowers to make the image look livelier. Some are superimposed over others to create highly expressive and juxtaposed areas of color. The colors range from carmine and cadmium red to more neutral greens, which logically pass through a wide range of yellows. There are also spots of color on the vase —notice the splashes of violet, ultramarine blue, cobalt blue, sienna and titanium white that almost make it look pointillist.

Fig. 6. The artist has added a new wash to the background. He has superimposed a new gray-blue wash, diluted in thinners, over the pink one he painted before. This, too, takes on the form of degradation. The bunch of flowers is now finished. Rather than being too detailed, the picture looks more like something out of the impressionist era. The artists adds a few pure white strokes to the vase to show where light is falling and uses a little more black to touch up the tripod that

4

5

TIPS

1-. Just like marble powder, sawdust offers different textures (from very smooth to very lumpy). Choose the right type for your picture, and do not be afraid to combine different types in the same piece.

2-. Sawdust can also be sprinkled over a surface covered with glue, although sand from a beach or river is usually preferable for this because sawdust tends to break up too easily.

1

2

supports it. There is no doubt that, considering how simple the piece is and how difficult it is to work on textures made using sawdust, the finished piece produces a surprising effect.

Oil painting with the encaustic technique

The next exercise is much more complex, but the results are excellent if everything is done properly. Óscar Sanchís is going to paint a view of the French town of Albi using the encaustic technique. Encaustic work involves mixing beeswax pigments and applying them to the surface when they are still warm. For this, you will need special tools (wax, a small stove, a large pot and another smaller one) and you will have to make a special palette that is suited to working with hot paint, because en-

caustic painting usually involves applying hot paints to a cold surface. A spatula is used to apply the paint to the support. Carefully follow these instructions and copy what the artist does.

Fig. 1. The artist gets straight down to work, without making a preparatory sketch. With small amounts of sienna, ultramarine blue, burnt umber and

cadmium yellow he starts outlining the picture. When paint is hot, the different colors can be dragged over each other to produce strange effects. But as soon as the spatula leaves its mark on the cold surface of the support, the wax solidifies. You need to work quickly.

Fig. 2. Paint is normally applied as short pastes. The very nature of the medium does not lend itself to long, fluid lines, and that is why we use a spatula. A little ultramarine blue mixed with white is used for the water in the river and then new violet pastes are added to the center of the painting. It is not hard to manipulate the spatula and it can leave marks that are just as rich as those you would make with a brush, but they do, of course, look very different. As you can see, the different elements of the painting are still unclear, but as we make smaller spatula marks, the different features will start appearing.

Fig. 3. For these opening stages, short splashes of color have been used to apply relatively dark tones. Now, we add a few spots of light using a cadmium yellow, which we will be working on a little more as part of the next step. Notice that the silhouettes of the cathedral and the group of houses are now more compact. The sky is painted with ultramarine blue, a touch of carmine and plenty of white. The shape of the clouds is made by press-

MODELS

1-. *Side street in Pals* by Ester Llaudet (artist's private collection). The encaustic approach is ideal for the natural textures of rocks, making a broken, granulated surface. If you look closely, you will see that there is a rich variety of different colors in each paste, which is what causes that characteristic finish.

3

ing the flat edge of the spatula onto the paint while it is still hot. If you want to mold the wax, use one of your hands while the other holds a hot hairdryer.

Fig. 4. The main spots of light are now applied to the facades on the left with warm colors, derived from mix-

tures of different parts of sienna, yellow ochre and burnt umber. Notice how they contrast with what is a predominantly cold colored image. Two varieties of blue appear in the river, and you can now make out the silhouette of the arches in the bridge. At this stage, the painting clearly looks

4

TIPS

1-. There used to be such things as thermal palettes that were specially designed for encaustic painting, but nowadays they are hard to find in the shops. But it is quite easy to make a home-made one – just find a rectangular sheet of iron or steel and lay it over a few candles. The metal should be about two inches away from the source of heat.

2-. There are several types of wax to choose from, and preferences vary. Personally, I would go for a block of natural beeswax because it tends not to have so much affect on the colors of light pigments.

1

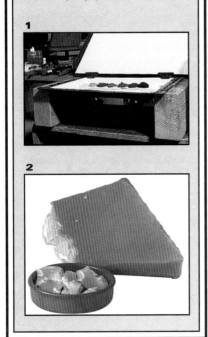

2

quite expressionist.

Fig. 5. Keep painting the area that corresponds to the river. At this point you need to put away the spatula you have been using up until now and use a smaller one to specify more concrete details. Start molding the forms of the arches under the bridge using

5

cadmium yellow and ochre where it is lighter and black, sienna, violet and burnt umber for the darker parts of the bridge. An encaustic painting like this is characterized by a strong dependence on the image as a whole in which no one stroke is more important than any other.

Fig. 6. Now we need to go back to the lighter tones and the areas of light, such as, for example, those that appear under the arches of the bridge. To do this you need to add a paste of ochre, burnt umber and a touch of cadmium red to the previous tones. The artist accentuates the water in the river in a similar way, putting sparkles of a lighter blue in the lower right hand section of the picture. The way you use color in an encaustic painting is decisive, you cannot make particularly defined edges with this technique, rather you will have to work with blurred and inaccurate forms.

Fig. 7. Now you need to use a synthetic brush to apply a few dark tones that will suggest the openings in the facades such as doors, lintels and windows. These features look some-

6

TIPS

3-. Melt the wax in a double saucepan over a stove, but always have the palette close at hand. Pick up the wax with a teaspoon and mix it with pigments over the palette. The quantity of pigment depends on how opaque you want the mixture to be.

4-. If you want to rectify any part of the painting surface when it has already dried, you need to warm the area with a hot rod or hairdryer and then remove any excess paint or just modify the original texture.

3

4

what pointillist, having been painted with thick touches of color. To paint a piece like this successfully, you need to know how to combine shaded areas with lines to put variety into the image. The artist has to know exactly

7

how much detail is needed, and should not spoil all that he has done by superimposing too many colors.

Fig. 8. The final state of the painting speaks for itself. This is an extraordinarily fine piece of work. The accumulative effects of the short, direct strokes, which consolidate the lines around each shape, create an attractive and surprisingly direct image. If you look carefully, you will see that each paste includes the wide variety of colors that produce that unique textured quality of encaustic paintings. It is an arduous process, but if you have managed to follow this exercise all the way through without making any mistakes, there is no reason why you can't produce a painting that is just as good.

8

MODELS **²**

2-. *There's always a piece that doesn't fit* by Teresa Trol (artist's private collection). The artist used the encaustic technique to paint this figure. The flesh colored tones are solid and pasty. After blending the whole surface, the head is merged into other areas with the point of an electric soldering iron. The illustration shows how the strokes mixed with the circular marks left by the tool suggest the textures of the clothing on the right arm.

Creating volumes with paper

In the next exercise, Bibiana Crespo is going to model the volume of the elements of this still life with paper (fig. 0). After configuring the relief of the picture, she will use oil paints to give the image a brighter, livelier finish. This exercise will show how you do not need to paint objects and forms in too much detail –the volume of the paper and the context will provide enough information for the spectator to understand the details

without actually having to define forms or figurative objects. This kind of still life is ideal for decorating a kitchen.

Fig. 1. We start by drawing the pencilled outline of the model on a support made of gray cardboard (like the

1

ones that bookbinders use). To create the volume of the different elements, we use newspaper. Crumple up small pieces of paper into little balls and

stick them to the support with latex or carpenter's glue. Start by modeling the string of garlic that crosses the composition diagonally and then fill the spaces with the remaining shapes. It is important that the outside of the paper is firmly pressed down to get rid of any air pockets. You do not need to represent any of the forms too perfectly; it is enough to simply suggest their volumes.

Fig. 2. As we stick the different shapes onto the gray cardboard, we need to squash them down so that they are firmly stuck on. When the glue feels dry, use a shaving brush or a synthetic brush to paste a layer of latex over the shapes. Now carefully put one or more pieces of tissue paper over the whole surface as if it were a layer of skin, and press the tissue down so that it molds itself over the forms that the paper describes. The artist now applies another layer of latex and water to make sure it is resistant. She now leaves everything for a few hours as she waits for it to dry out before she can start painting.

Fig. 3. There are two ways of painting. You can either start with the background and move on to the nearer planes, or you do what the artist

MODELS

1-. *Waterfall* by Grau Carod (artist's private collection). The technique of crumpling up paper to form small lumps and bas-reliefs is ideal for reproducing rocks. It is a popular technique for putting more volume into the objects that are nearer to the spectator. The irregularities in the surface of the paper help to recreate the texture of rocks.

3

form strokes without going over the edges of any of the objects. The strokes should be practically unnoticeable. There are two values used for the pepper –the first is darker and is made of an intense permanent green (taken straight from the tube), and the second is lighter and is made by adding cadmium yellow to the previous green. The mixture is made on the support itself using plenty of thick paint so that the strokes look irregular and grooved. The turnip is painted with different ochre tones, which should either be lightened with thinners or a little white paint.

Fig. 5. The rest of the vegetables are painted with more carefree strokes. The texture is insinuated with different tones of the same

does and start with the molded forms, generally the nearer elements, and leave the background for later. If we do the latter, we begin with a thick layer of paint over the nearer objects. The color used is a mixture of carmine and ultramarine blue, with the former being used in the greater proportion. With a very diluted ochre, paint the string of garlic using little more than two values –an medium intensity ochre for the shadowed area and ochre mixed with white for the lighter area.

Fig. 4. Now work on the vegetables with greens and ochres combined with cadmium reds and earth colors, using uni-

4

color range and the forms can be as rough as you like, often consisting of random strokes with little apparent meaning. The legs of ham are painted with freer lines and juxtaposed shades of pink, ochre, sienna, raw umber and orange. The volume of the elements is insinuated by the presence of brighter tones on the more prominent sections of the relief.

Fig. 6. The main elements have now been painted in their corresponding

5

colors, and now all we need to do is outline a few color details and think about the chromatic harmony between each of the different shades, leaving the background until the end. The layout of the different shades is what makes each of the shapes recognizable. Compare the legs of ham and the leaves on the vegetables in this illustration to those in the previous one to get an idea of what the artist is doing. You will see how successively added shades of color define the final appearance of these objects. These new colors need to follow in logical succession, getting more and more elab-

6

orate as they near their definitive state. The original layers of color gradually disappear under the much thicker ones that are applied after.

Fig. 7. The background is painted with a very diluted ochre-gray, letting the color spread and form into patches. Colors depend on the positions of each of the objects in a still life. It would not make much sense to paint a distant plane, like this background, in bright colors. As we paint the background, we make a few modifications to the colors of the vegetables. The glows of light are painted with liberal strokes that do not mix with the earlier ones. There is a strong contrast between the different colors, and the artist makes clever use of the patterns caused by complementary contrast. Look at the intense con-

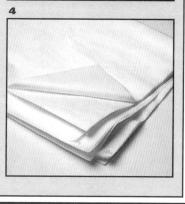
trast between the green on the vegetables and the red and orange on the tomatoes, peppers and oranges.

Fig. 8. Having covered the background, the final details include a few spots of cadmium red and raw umber in the bottom left hand section of the painting. To break the monotony of the space at the top the artist paints the foot of another leg of ham along

7

8

with two or three touches of dark gray. Now you just have to increase the contrasts progressively with small strokes that increase the tone and at the same time define the forms of the more distant planes in the still

life. If we want to portray a sense of depth, it is important that the colors of the elements seen in the relief in the foreground are painted with more intense colors than those that were used for the background, and the details need to be much clearer and more contrasted.

MODELS

2

2-. *Still life with flowers* by Josep Antoni Domingo (artist's private collection). Just like many other materials, paper can be used for recreating volumes and textures to get a better likeness. Compare how it has been crumpled and torn to represent flowers with the flatter more rounded way that it is used for the fruit and the basket.

Molding with plaster

This time, we are going to work with the painter and illustrator Josep Antoni Domingo, using the plastering technique to model textures. Plaster is used in a similar way to marble powder, but as it is a more malleable material, you can model forms much more accurately. Without further ado, let's see how he does it. The chosen subject is going to be this Indian landscape that combines rocks, trees and buildings –a rich variety of textures that are highly appropriate for producing interesting effects. As usual, you should try to copy what the artist does.

Fig. 1. First of all, mix the plaster with water and spread the paste over the surface of the support, which should be rigid enough not to warp when such a damp material is applied to it. Now press down on the surface with a spatula to mold the forms of the landscape. You can create quite irregular, ran-

dom forms by applying more paste with the spatula, by combing the surface into straight and wavy lines, or stroking it with a cloth or a hard brush. Compare the photograph to the plastered surface. Notice that the slopes and scraped sections correspond to those in the original image.

Fig. 2. Once the model has been shaped in all of the right places, leave the plaster to dry for a couple of hours. You will then be able to start applying the first layers of color. Like any good landscapists, Josep Antoni Domingo starts with the sky. He uses an ultramarine blue that he grays slightly with a touch of ochre. Notice that the ultramarine blue is purer nearer to the top and gets paler as it approaches the mountains. He has colored the most of the sky, but notice that he has left a few areas blank,

MODELS

1-. *View of a lake* by Josep Antoni Domingo (artist's private collection). The mountain slopes have first been shaped with plaster. The sky and the surface of the water have been left flat, so the contrasts between the different areas of the picture are even stronger. The soft plastered surface makes it far easier to paint minute details, unlike the far rougher surfaces made using materials such as marble powder or sawdust.

3

these spaces being reserved for the clouds later on. The sky plays an important role in any landscape. Not only does it determine light, shadow and contrast, but also the harmonic range of colors that appear in the image.

Fig. 3. New colors, well diluted in thinners, are used to mold the forms of the clouds. With a little ochre mixed with a touch of cadmium red and yellow, the artist applies the first values. The mountainside, which makes up the foreground, is painted with different shades of ochre. Simi-

larly, different shades of permanent green, cadmium green and emerald green are mixed directly onto the support to paint the vegetation. The texture of the vegetation is quite unlike that of the rocky mountain slopes, and needs to be painted in a different way, using pointillism to insinuate the effect that is produced by the contrast between light and shadow in the leaves of the trees.

Fig. 4. The process continues and the artist keeps spreading washes over the whole surface of the painting. As you can see, the treatment is occa-

4

TIPS

1-. To prepare the paste, mix powdered plaster, which you can buy at any hardware store, in a bowl of water. When the mixture has formed a paste, you can apply it to canvas.

2-. Try to create the textures and effects you need while the paste is still wet. Once it is dry and hard the only way of modifying the surface is by scraping at it with a sharp object, but in doing this you are running of the risk of breaking or cracking the solid surface.

1

2

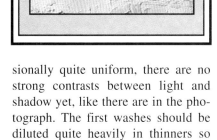

sionally quite uniform, there are no strong contrasts between light and shadow yet, like there are in the photograph. The first washes should be diluted quite heavily in thinners so that the color gets into the cracks,

5

making the textural effect produced by the plaster even more powerful. The quality of the texture may look even better if your next colors are applied as veils, because thick, dense colors take away a lot of its impact. But there are no strict rules in the world of art, and you are free to experiment with whatever methods you like.

Fig. 5. The artist adds sienna to the original ochre to accentuate contrasts. You can see the first areas of shadows are appearing. Notice that the transition between light and shadow is not an abrupt one, rather it is gradual, forming a tonal gradation. Lightening sienna with a little thinners and white paint, paint the castle walls; for the time being just sketch a couple of values to suggest its volume. Look how strong the contrasts are between the vegetation in the center of the image and the ochre colored mountain. This helps clarify the outline and shape of the trees. Complementary colors are a very useful resource in this respect.

Fig. 6. Now you need to put aside your larger brushes and move on to using a medium, round brush. First, we work on the castle using large

3

4

quantities of sienna mixed with ochre to blend the colors of the walls together. Work on the mountainsides in a similar way, gradually covering all of the remaining blank spaces. The only spaces you should not paint are those that will be used for painting the buildings. Paint shadows over

6

7

shadowed face of the castle with more violet colors and use the same color to touch up the mountain slopes. You can paint much more accurate details on the smoother plastered surface than you were able to do on marble powder.

Fig. 8. If you study this illustration of the finished picture, you will see how thin and detailed the strokes are. The paint is not very thick, just enough to alter the tones of the previous layers. For this final stage, most of the attention has been given to the mountain slopes, with tiny touches of color being used to suggest the cracks and lumps on the rocky surface. To finish, add a few touches of white mixed with small quantities of sienna and ochre to suggest areas of light on the

these areas, using short strokes and touches of gray-blue, not unlike those that we used to paint the sky earlier on. Finish off the shadows with ochre strokes that have been lightened with white and dirtied with gray.

Fig. 7. Now you need to use your smallest brushes to paint the details. The artist uses a sable brush to paint the accurate details on the facades of the houses, the textures of the vegetation and the craggy rocks on the mountain slopes. Add more violet and raw umber tones to the group of houses to indicate where the streets are. Paint the background area under the horizon, just left of center, with bluer, less defined tones. Paint the

8

castle walls and the mountainsides. And with that, the painting is finished.

MODELS

2

2-. *Woodland clearing* by Grau Carod (artist's private collection). Plastered textures are perfect for painting scenes like this where there is a lot of vegetation. The end of the spatula can be used to mold the tensions and effects in the texture of the branches. Now, with liberal and generous applications of color, you can brighten up the picture with dynamic forms like these.

Garden with silicon

For the last exercise in this book, we are going to be using a far less common technique. I certainly do not know of any professional artist who regularly creates volumes with silicon combined with oil paints. This technique would come under the heading of extracted painting, which involves applying streaks of paint that come directly from the tube and are left to dry on the surface of the support. For this exercise, we are once again going to be working with Óscar Sanchís, who is going to be painting the corner of this typical patio in Seville, Spain (fig. 0). As a support he will simply be using paper stuck to a rigid board.

Fig. 1. The artist starts with a detailed analysis of the model and he decides how he is going to interpret the plants, arches and flower pots in a design based around streaks of silicon. When he is ready, he sketches a simple outline on the paper, takes a silicon spray gun and starts applying the paste along the lines that he drew earlier.

As he draws, he adds a few small textures and random touches that make the area of vegetation more attractive. Fig. 2. The paste needs to dry for a couple of days before he can start using paints. Once everything is dry to the touch, he starts applying the first layers of color. The paint needs to be diluted in plenty of thinners, because the way in which silicon slightly rejects oil paint diluted in thinners produces curious effects. The artist works on the main areas of vegetation, such as the ivy that covers the arches and patio walls from top to

0

bottom, which is painted with cadmium yellow, emerald green, permanent green and a touch of burnt umber. The colors are applied to the support directly so that each one blends into the others.

Fig. 3. To cover the floor, the artist uses a mixture of sienna, ochre, yellow, cadmium red and touches of white and gray. See how the proportions vary and the paint is much thicker than in the previous phase. Thick and only very lightly diluted oil paint covers the silicon surface in an opaque way. With the same colors that were used at the bottom of the painting, a few strokes have been added at the top to suggest the ledges, windows and a few grooved marks that represent the leaves of the trees.

Fig. 4. The technique of combining oil paints with silicon gives the artist the opportunity to work freely and without inhibitions. Silicon paste is so malleable that the surface can be worked with a spatula, a rubber tipped brush, a dirty piece of cloth, any type of brush or even manipulated with one's own fingertips. You will find that silicon feels has an elastic, soft and spongy feel to it. As it is not

MODEL

1

1-. *The boats* by Óscar Sanchís (artist's private collection). There are several ways of working with silicon, either pasting with a spatula or using the extracted technique (which involves applying streaks of paint to the outlines of each element). The former produces a more pasty surface, whereas the latter is more linear.

3

even slightly porous, you can easily modify what you have painted while the surface is still wet.

Fig. 5. Óscar Sanchís takes his brush again to clarify the images of the flowerpots. New strokes develop new textures and correct those that he made earlier. He touches them up until he is happy with their forms; then he uses a little red to paint the actual flowers. Short, pasty colors stop the colors below from interfering with or

5

dirtying his strokes. Although the strokes should be short, they should not be mere dots, and each area should include a pleasant range of tones, giving each stroke a different

4

shade and chromatic quality.

Fig. 6. Continue with small amounts of paint that finish forming the vegetation at the bottom of the patio. The trees gradually get thicker and thicker, the flowerpots are now quite clear, and so are the shadows that they cast across the patio floor. The artist keeps adding to the areas that are filled with plants, using small, pasty strokes that contrast with the lighter tones in the background. Small diagonal lines are used on the floor to help convey the

6

idea of space and depth of perspective in the image. And that is about it. Rather than risk spoiling things with too many details, the painting looks fresh and spontaneous if it is left just as it is.

Glossary

A

Agglutinate. Substance that is mixed with powdered pigment to make a medium of painting.

Alla prima. Direct painting technique that involves painting quickly in just one session and never going back over what one has painted.

B

Blending. Procedure that involves softening contours and areas of contact between colors to form gentle gradations.

C

Chiaroscuro. Rembrandt was a master of chiaroscuro. In his work, forms and colors are clearly visible despite being surrounded by intense shadows. In his books on painting, Parramón defines chiaroscuro as "the art of painting light over shadow".

Chromatic harmony. The balanced relationship of different colors within a painting.

Composition. The balanced and harmonized distribution of the different elements that appear in a picture. Composing involves bearing these factors in mind as one selects the best arrangements.

Covering capacity. The capacity that a color has to dominate other colors in mixtures and veils.

D

Degradation. Reducing the value of a tone, gradually making it more intense or softer, so that the transition is gradual rather than abrupt.

Dry brush. Painting technique that involves applying thick paint to the support, so that it sticks to both the pores in the canvas and the texture of the paint on the surface.

F

Film. Layer of paint or coating over the surface.

Fit. Preliminary drawing that establishes the basic structure of bodies as simple geometric forms (cubes, rectangles, prisms etc) that are often known as frames.

G

Genre. Classification of artistic techniques, such as still lives, landscapes, figures and interiors.

I

Induction of complementaries. A phenomenon derived from simultaneous contrasts, which complies with the norm that states that "to modify a particular color, you simply need to change the color that surrounds it".

L

Local color. The genuine color of an object when it is not affected by shadow, reflections or other factors.

M

Medium. Liquid in which pigments are held, for example linseed oil is used for oil paints and acrylic resin for acrylics. Pastel sticks can be mixed or dampened in any of these mediums.

Merging. Technique that involves spreading or reducing one or more layers of color onto a background layer, so that the lower layer is still visible through the superimposed one.

Mixed techniques. Using different painting procedures in the same picture, or using a combination of different supports.

Modeling

Modeling. Although this is a sculptural term, it can also be applied to painting and drawing to refer to the way in which different tones are applied to create an illusion of the third dimension.

O

Opacity. The capacity that a gray shade or wash has for covering a layer below it. Opacity varies from pigment to pigment.

Opaque painting technique. Pastel technique that involves applying thick layers of color to create a textured surface with little or no merging.

P

Pasting. Technique that involves applying thick layers of color to create textured surfaces.

Perspective. Way of representing the three-dimensional world on a two-dimensional surface.

Pigments. Coloring agents in powdered form that are obtained from natural sources (although some are now made synthetically) that, when mixed with an agglutinate, create paint.

Pointillism. Painting technique that involves applying small dots to the canvas.

Pre-painting. Preliminary paint that the rest of the colors of a piece are painted over.

Preparatory sketch. The preliminary stage in the construction of a drawing or painting, from which the definitive piece can be derived. Several sketches might be made before the artist decides upon the idea he wants to work with.

Primer. Adhesive or gelatinous material that is applied to the canvas before it is painted, making the support less absorbent. It can also be used as an agglutinate in paint.

Proportion. The relationship of one part with the tonality of a piece.

S

Saturation. Value or chromatic degree of a color. Strength of a color that a surface can reflect.

Sgraffito. Technique that involves scraping a layer of color with a sharp instrument, so that the color of the support becomes visible.

Solvents. Liquids used for dissolving oil paints. The solvent for water based colors is water and for oil based products, turpentine essence, thinners and similar substances are used.

Stanley Knife. Sharp knife used for cutting paper, made up of a metal blade inside a plastic handle.

Style. In sculpture, drawing and painting, this is the way that the task is approached. It can be agitated, brusque, delicate, slow, fast... It determines the manner of working of each individual artist.

Support. Surface used for painting or drawing, such a board, sheet of paper or canvas.

T

Texture. Tactile and visual quality of the surface of a drawing or painting. It can be smooth, granulated, rough or cracked.

Tonal background. Opaque coloring in which the color is mixed with white to spread the color in a uniform way. A tonal background can also be colored. Tonal color. Color offered by the shadow of objects.

Tone. Term that has its origins in music that, when applied to art, refers to the strength and relief of all the parts of a painting with respect to light and color.

Transparency. Way of applying color so that light or the previous layer of color filters through.

V

Value. As much in drawing as painting, volume or modeling is obtained from the tonal values of the model. At the same time, it is achieved through the comparison and tonal resolution of effects of light and shadow.

Veils. Layers of transparent color that are superimposed over the preliminary color when it is dry.

Viscosity. Measure of the characteristic fluidity of a color or medium.

Volatility. Evaporation potential of a solution.

Volume. Three-dimensional effect of a model in the two-dimensional space of a painting.

W

Wet on wet painting. Technique that involves painting over an area of recently applied paint while it is still damp. The level of dampness can be controlled, depending on the effect that the artist wishes to create.

Whiting. Ground, washed chalk that is used for priming cloth and in the composition of pastels.

Acknowledgements

The author would like to thank the following people and companies for their help in publishing this volume of the *Effects and tricks* series. Gabriel Martín Roig for helping with the writing and the general coordination of the book; Antonio Oromí for his photography; Vicenç Piera of the Piera company for advice and orientation concerning painting and drawing materials and utensils; Manel Úbeda of the Novasis company for their help with the edition and production of the photosetting and photostatting; Olga Bernard, Bibiana Crespo, Amin Idrissi, Carlant, Óscar Sanchís and Eva M.ª Durán for granting us permission to use several photographs that were used as models for painting, and a special thanks to the artistsTeresa Trol, Josep Antoni Domingo, Sofía Isus, Bibiana Crespo, Grau Carod, Carlant and Óscar Sanchís.